W9-AOA-112

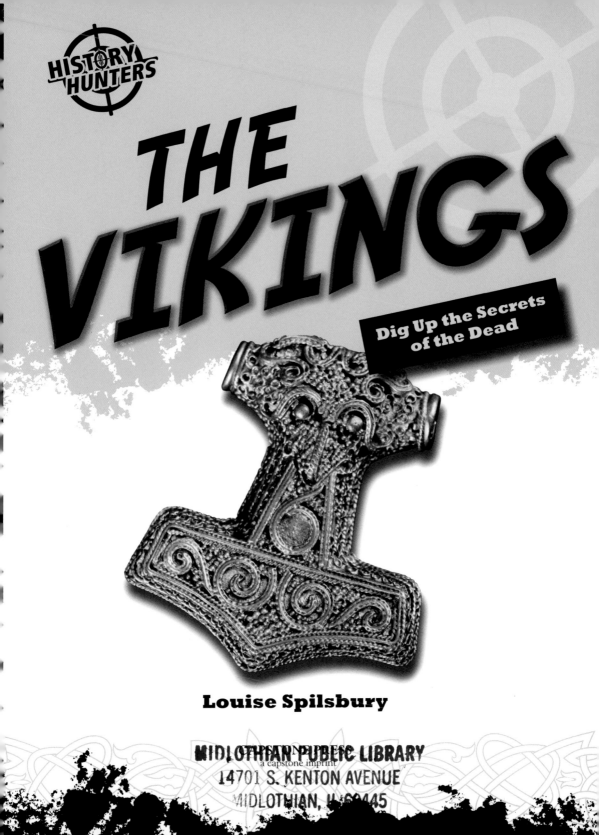

THE VIKINGS

Dig Up the Secrets of the Dead

Louise Spilsbury

MIDLOTHIAN PUBLIC LIBRARY
a capstone imprint

Produced for Capstone by Calcium
Edited by Sarah Eason and Jennifer Sanderson
Designed by Paul Myerscough
Picture research by Rachel Blount
Consultant: John Malam
Production by Paul Myerscough
Originated by Calcium Creative Limited © 2016
Printed and bound in China

20 19 18 17 16
10 9 8 7 6 5 4 3 2 1

Library of Congress Cataloging-in-Publication Data
Hardback ISBN 978 1 5157 2552 7
e-book ISBN 978 1 5157 2558 9

Acknowledgments
The author and publisher are grateful to the following for permission to reproduce copyright material: Getty
Images pp. 18 (Werner Forman), 22 (Print Collector); Shutterstock cover (Roman Kaplanski), pp. 1 (Kachalkina
Veronika), 4 (Voyagerix), 5 (NERYX.COM), 6 (Dave Head), 9 (Kachalkina Veronika), 10 (InavanHateren), 12
(Valeriiaarnaud), 13 (Roman Kaplanski), 14 (Sergei Afanasev), 17 (Kachalkina Veronika), 19 (Popova Valeriya),
24 (Jps), 25 (Iakov Filimonov), 26 (Kachalkina Veronika), 28 (Thomas Males); Wikimedia Commons pp. 7
(Berig), 8 (Berig), 11 (Kim Traynor), 15 (Wolfgang Sauber), 16 (Jeblad), 20 (Thorguds), 21 (JMiall), 23 (Steven
G. Johnson), 27 (Bloodofox), 29 (The National Museum of Denmark).

Every effort has been made to contact copyright holders of material reproduced in this book. Any omissions will be
rectified in subsequent printings if notice is given to the publisher.

All the Internet addresses (URLs) given in this book were valid at the time of going to press. However, due to the
dynamic nature of the Internet, some addresses may have changed, or sites may have changed or ceased to exist
since publication. While the author and publisher regret any inconvenience this may cause readers, no responsibility
for any such changes can be accepted by either the author or the publisher.

CONTENTS

Throughout the book you will find Deadly
Secrets boxes that show an historical object.
Use the clues and the hint in these boxes to
figure out what the object is or what it was
used for. Then check out the Answer box at the
bottom of the page to see if you are right.

THE VIKINGS

The Vikings came from an area in northern Europe known as **Scandinavia**. Early Vikings were peaceful people. They were farmers and fishermen, living off the land and the cold waters of their home.

In CE 700, when they could no longer survive on their own land, they set off in ships to search for new lands in which to live. They became explorers, and fierce, **plundering** warriors. They terrified people and killed those who stood in their way. Eric Bloodaxe, Ivar the Boneless, Ragnar Shaggy-Trousers, and Thorstein the Black are some of history's most famous Vikings.

The Vikings came from the countries we now call Denmark, Norway, and Sweden.

Running Amok Among the Monks

The Vikings' first successful raid was in CE 793, when they attacked the Christian **monastery** at Lindisfarne in Northumbria, in northern England. **Monks** were easy targets. They had no weapons and they did not fight back. The Vikings burned buildings. They killed the monks or chased them into the sea to drown. They stole treasures such as gold, silver, jewels, and books. After this, they set out to raid places throughout Europe.

The word "Viking" comes from the Old **Norse** word for a pirate raid.

Secrets of the Dead

Why the Vikings Set Off on Raids

- Better land: The land in Scandinavia was tough to farm because it was either too hilly, covered in forests, or too sandy. Many Vikings left in search of better land on which to grow crops and rear their cows, sheep, and pigs.
- More land: When a father died, the family farm passed down to the eldest son. Some younger men did not want to just work for their older brothers. They wanted land of their own. As there was a shortage of good land in Scandinavia, they had to go elsewhere to find it.
- Treasure: The Vikings also wanted treasure—and lots of it.

5

DIGGING UP
THE PAST

Most of what we know about the Vikings comes from under the ground. Graves tell us a lot about how they lived because Vikings were usually buried with their belongings. **Archaeologists** have found jewelry, weapons, and furniture. They have also found **bronze** and silver bowls and knives in Viking graves.

These **artifacts** have survived because Viking craftsmen made them out of long-lasting materials such as stone, metal, bone, and hardwood that do not rot easily. Archaeologists have also found woolen clothes that were preserved in frozen soil for hundreds of years. Using these pieces of evidence, archaeologists can figure out how the Vikings lived. They can also tell what they wore and some of the things they believed in.

The treasures the Vikings stole from **abbeys** across Britain and Ireland tell us where they raided and when.

How We Know Vikings Were Also Victims

In 2009, road builders digging up an old quarry pit in Dorset, England, found about 50 skeletons. By studying their teeth, experts realized that the mass grave contained Viking men. They were mostly aged 18 to 25 years and they had all been executed. Their heads had been cut off and piled up on one side. The experts dated the site as being from CE 970–1025. This tells us that they could have been victims of an order given by Saxon King Ethelred the Unready in CE 1002 to kill Vikings who were in England at that time.

Picture Stones

Vikings also carved pictures into large slabs of stone up to 13 feet (4 meters) high. These are shaped like a keyhole and look a little like giant comic strips. Picture stones are carved with images that show buildings, people, objects, and landscapes. They have images of Viking gods and kings that tell us about their beliefs and **rituals**.

Vikings put up picture stones to remember important Vikings after they died. They also marked the boundaries of a family's land. Picture stones were sometimes placed near graves or more often, by pathways where people would see them regularly.

This picture is one of the famous Stora Hammars stones from Sweden. It shows warriors, weapons, horses, and Viking ships.

GRUESOME GODS AND LUCKY CHARMS

Vikings believed that their many gods lived in a kingdom in the sky called Asgard. Asgard was connected to Midgard (the Earth) by a rainbow bridge.

One-eyed Odin was the god of wisdom and war. He was in charge of the other gods. He rode around on an eight-legged horse named Sleipnir. Odin knew everything that went on in both worlds thanks to his two black ravens, Memory and Thought. They flew around and told Odin everything they had seen.

Gods and Battles

The Vikings told stories about the wild adventures of their gods and goddesses. Evil giants, dark elves, and dwarves also lived in Midgard. The gods fought these giants and evil forces. Vikings believed that the world would end with one dreadful, final battle between the gods and the giants. Viking chiefs acted as priests to lead Viking rituals at stone **altars** in great halls. They also sometimes threw **offerings** of weapons, jewelry, and tools into lakes for the gods.

This picture stone shows Odin on his magical horse named Sleipnir (top right). Sleipnir means "the sliding one." Some experts believe that this picture stone shows Odin arriving at the world of the dead.

DEADly Secrets

This is a Viking **amulet** in the shape of Thor's hammer. All over the Viking world, many people wore amulets like these, especially those Vikings who went to sea. What do you think an amulet is?

Hint: Seas were rough and Vikings needed all the luck they could get when on their ships. ● ● ● ● ● ● ● ● ●

Secrets of the Dead

Viking Gods and Goddesses

- Thor: Thor was the powerful god of thunder. Vikings believed a flash of lightning meant that Thor had flung his hammer, which he used to protect the gods against the giants.
- Freya: Freya was the goddess of love and marriage. One of her vehicles was a chariot drawn by cats.
- Loki: Loki was the god of tricks. He changed into many different forms to carry out his mischief.

Answer: An amulet is a lucky charm. Amulets with Thor's hammer were very popular because Vikings believed he and his hammer could protect them from harm.

FIERY FUNERALS
AND SCARY SACRIFICES

Viking warriors were fearless. They flung themselves into battle as if they had nothing to lose. They believed that warriors who died in battle would spend the **afterlife** feasting at a long table in a paradise called Valhalla, inside Asgard.

Viking ships were so important that after great warriors died, they were buried in boats or boat-shaped graves. These were covered with earth mounds. Often they were marked with huge stones that formed the shape of a boat, called a stone ship. Sometimes, an important leader would be placed on his ship. The ship was then set alight and allowed to drift out to sea. His people would watch from the shore.

Graves were often covered by stones in the shape of the hull of a ship. This is because the Vikings wanted to give dead people a ship for their journey to the afterlife.

Objects for the Afterlife

All Vikings believed they would pass into another world after death. Everyone was buried with some of their belongings, to take into the afterlife. Men were buried with around one-third of their belongings. These included money, tools, clothing, and weapons. Women were buried with things people thought they would need, such as needles and thread and cooking pots. Pet dogs, horses, and even **slaves** were sometimes **sacrificed** to go with important leaders to the next world.

The items that archaeologists find buried with dead Vikings reveal an enormous amount about Viking life.

Secrets of the Dead

The Oseberg Mystery

A secret was buried with the Oseberg ship in Norway. Inside it were the bodies of two women, one aged about 70 and the other 50, who died in around CE 784. Buried with them were many riches, including horse sleighs, a decorated chariot, and beautiful woven tapestries. There were also the bones of 14 or 15 horses, a cat, birds, a bull, a cow, and four dogs. The women must have been important. Maybe one was a queen or a religious leader. Was the other woman a slave sacrificed to go with her owner to the afterlife? We may never know.

SENSATIONAL SHIPS AND DRAGON HEADS

One of the secrets to the Vikings' success was the design of their ships. Their lightweight, speedy longships survived the stormy seas of the North Atlantic Ocean. They were shallow enough to carry warriors up rivers to raid inland villages.

A Viking longship was about 98 feet (30 m) long. It carried 60 men. Large sails powered these sensational ships. When the wind dropped, the Vikings rowed their ships swiftly along using long wooden oars.

Boat Building

Viking ships were built from long planks of wood. These were joined together with wooden pegs and iron nails. The wooden planks on the side of the hull overlapped each other. This made the ship very strong. Viking shipbuilders worked alongside a river or near a sea. This meant that they could slide the ship straight into the water on top of long logs.

Viking shipbuilders made the longships watertight by filling spaces between the planks with wool, moss, or animal hair, mixed with tar or animal fat.

DEADly Secrets

At the front end of a Viking longship there was often a carved, wooden **figurehead** in the shape of a frightening creature, such as a dragon. That is why longships were often known as dragon ships. What do you think these figureheads were for?

Hint: Dragons are not known for being friendly or gentle.

Secrets of the Dead

The Parts of a Viking Longship

- Sail: Viking longships had one large, square sail made of wool. It was often brightly colored with stripes or diamond patterns.
- Rudder: The large rudder at the back was used for steering. One man controlled it.
- Oars: Ships had up to 50 oars. When rowing, Vikings sat on wooden boxes that held their belongings because most ships did not have benches. They pulled in the oars when the sail was in use and covered the oar holes with little wooden panels to keep water from pouring in.
- Keel: This was like the backbone of the boat. It was made from the long trunk of an oak tree.

Answer: Vikings used dragon figureheads on the prow, or front, of their ships to scare their enemies.

13

LONG VOYAGES AND TERRIFYING RAIDS

A dragon ship usually arrived in a new land at dawn. This was the best time for a surprise attack. The Viking warriors jumped out as soon as their ship touched land, shouting battle cries and calling on their gods to help them.

They rampaged through houses, killing many villagers while they slept. They would take some villagers as slaves. After filling their ships with all the loot they could carry, they climbed aboard and made a quick getaway.

This is a modern copy of a Viking longship. Longships were powered by oars or by the wind. The ship's single, large, square sail was tied up when not in use.

DEADly Secrets

This is a Viking shield. Shields were made of wood. Often, they had pieces of iron across the front to strengthen them. They were handmade and painted. Many shields were attached to the sides of a ship. Why do you think this was?

Hint: The ships pulled right up onto land so Vikings could jump out and fight immediately.

Life on Board

At sea, Vikings ate only cold and dried food, such as meat and fish, because they could not risk a fire on a wooden boat. They carried supplies of water, beer, or sour milk to drink. If they were lucky, they slept in woolen tents on shore at night. They lit fires to cook food and keep warm. More often, they slept at sea on the hard wooden deck under blankets or furs. If the weather was really bad, they laid the sail over the boat to make a sort of tent to sleep under.

Secrets of the Dead

How Vikings Navigated

- Vikings sailed close to the coast as far as possible, watching for landmarks.
- In open water, they looked at the position of the Sun, and the stars in the sky to help them **navigate**.
- They looked out for birds. Seabirds are known to head toward land at the end of the day.

Answer: The Vikings' round shields were hooked onto the side of a ship because this was a good place to store them on a voyage. It also kept them nearby so warriors could grab them quickly if there was a fight.

FIERCE WARRIORS AND DEADLY WEAPONS

A gang of Vikings running toward a village must have been a terrifying sight. As the Vikings shouted and roared, people could see their teeth filed into sharp points and rubbed with red berry juice to make them look even more fearsome.

Vikings wielded dangerous weapons such as axes, knives, and spears with iron tips. Their sharp, double-edged swords were so deadly that the Vikings often gave them names, such as Viper, Gnawer, Hole-maker, and Leg-biter.

Real Viking helmets did not have horns! They were made of iron hammered into a bowl or cone shape that fitted snugly over the head. Some were lined with animal fur.

Secrets of the Dead

Vikings that Went Berserk

The word berserk (meaning out of control) comes from the Viking word for fierce warriors who fought in an uncontrollable fury. At that time, "berserker" meant bearskin because these warriors fought wearing wolf or bear skins. They howled like wild animals. Berserkers believed they did not need to wear battle armor because Odin, the god of war, gave them super-powers.

DEADly Secrets

Viking swords were very strong and sharp because they were made of steel. Vikings made steel by adding carbon (from charcoal) to iron. Warriors carried swords in a leather holder hanging from the waist. This meant they could be pulled out quickly in a fight. Most swords have been found only in the graves of kings and warriors. Why do you think that is?

Hint: Only the very best would do for a Viking leader's burial.

Warrior Clothing

Viking warriors did not wear uniforms. Some wore padded leather shirts for protection. Richer Vikings had heavy chain mail jackets made from interlocking metal rings. Some Vikings wore iron helmets. These were made from a solid piece of metal with an extra piece that came down over the forehead. This protected the eyes and nose. Most men had only their wooden shields for protection. These had an iron handle at the back, which they also used for hitting people!

Answer: The chief of a tribe would be buried with his most prized possessions, including his sword. Steel swords were more precious and were carried only by kings and warriors. Ordinary Vikings carried knives or axes made of wood and iron.

POWERFUL KINGS AND SUFFERING SLAVES

There were three kinds of Viking: thralls, karls, and jarls. Thralls were the slaves. They were owned by karls and jarls. They did most of the hard work and the worst, dirtiest jobs.

The karls were ordinary folk like farmers, craftsmen, **blacksmiths**, and hunters. They could own a plot of land. They joined raiding parties in spring and summer to try to get treasure. The jarls were the wealthy nobles. They owned many slaves, land, ships, and farms. The strongest, richest, and most respected jarls could become a powerful leader or king, and boss everyone else around.

This picture shows the famous blonde Viking, King Harald Fairhair. He is shown freeing the giant Dofri. Dofri then helped him become the first king of Norway.

Sorry Slaves

Slaves, or thralls, could be bought and sold like property at the market. They were sometimes even sacrificed after their master died. This allowed them to continue to serve their master in the afterlife. If slaves did not behave properly, they were beaten. Owners could punish their slaves as much as they wanted. Slaves that tried to run away were captured and often killed. Slaves could get married and have families. If they sold things they made in their free time, they could even buy their freedom.

This man is using tools that were once used by a Viking blacksmith. Blacksmiths were important Viking karls because they made metal weapons and tools.

Secrets of the Dead

Where Viking Slaves Came From

- Most slaves were people captured in Viking raids. They were taken back to Viking villages wearing iron collars and chains.
- Some slaves were criminals. Crimes such as murder and theft were punished with slavery. If someone stole something, their punishment might be to become the slave of the person they robbed.
- People could be born slaves. If a child's mother and father were slaves, the child became a slave, too. If the child's mother was a slave but the father was a free man, the child grew up free, too.

TRADING GOODS AND STEALING SILVER

Early Viking visits to different countries ended in stealing, burning, and killing. As time went on, Vikings began to trade with other peoples. Viking cargo ships were called knarrs. Knarrs were slower and wider than longships. They had a space in the middle of the decking to store goods. Vikings sat at the ends of the ship to row it.

Vikings traveled all over Europe and as far east as central Asia, buying and selling a variety of goods. They also collected luxury items to fill the homes of the jarls.

Trading Bones and Birds

Products that the Vikings used to pay for their goods included things such as wood for shipbuilding and iron for tools. They sold **natural resources** from Scandinavia such as reindeer antlers and whalebones. They also sold walrus and **narwhal ivory** (tusks) for carving, the furs and skins of animals such as fox and otter, and, sometimes, live falcons. Vikings bought and sold slaves wherever they went.

This is a decorative handle on a well-preserved bucket that was found with other household items in the Oseberg ship. Vikings probably raided this beautifully made treasure from Irish monasteries in the eighth century.

DEADly Secrets

Before they made their own coins, Vikings often paid for goods using pieces of chopped up silver and other people's coins. This was known as hack silver. They paid for things in hack silver by weight so traders carried a pair of scales with them to figure out what to pay. Why do you think it was called "hack silver"?

Hint: Vikings had to share loot they had stolen in raids.

Secrets of the Dead

Where Treasures Came From

- Wine and wine jugs from France
- Silver coins from England and Ireland
- Swords from Germany
- Beautiful patterned silks from Persia (Iran)
- Silver, silk, and spices from Russia
- Glass and marble tiles from Italy
- Amber, a **fossilized resin** that was used to make beads, pendants, and brooches, from eastern Europe

Answer: Vikings shared the loot from their raids by hacking (chopping) it up into pieces and weighing it. It was used for trade or melted down to make something new.

CLOSE FAMILIES AND BLOOD FEUDS

Many Vikings that reached new lands decided to stay and settle in them peacefully. Soon, Viking villages and farms were found from Ireland, England, and Scotland to France and Russia. Families worked hard. Men farmed, made crafts, or went raiding or trading. Women looked after the home and children. They made clothes and looked after the land when their husbands were away.

Viking children did not go to school. They stayed at home and worked with their parents. Families often played a game similar to chess, called "hnefatafl," in which they moved pieces around a board of squares.

These grumpy-looking characters are pieces from a chess set used by Vikings. Most of the pieces are made from ivory from walrus tusks.

Problem Solving

Vikings made decisions about **blood feuds**, laws, and other important matters at meetings called Things—this is how the English word "thing" developed. Everyone in the village got together in a special place outside, often on a hill, to settle problems, and punish criminals. Viking laws were not written down. Everyone knew them because they went to Things, or heard about them from other people. Those who broke Viking laws were usually put to death.

DEADly Secrets

Vikings loved outdoor games and sports. Viking men liked swimming and horse racing. They made skis for sliding over the snow. Have you got any idea what sport they used these objects for?

Hint: Nervous Vikings often got "cold feet" about doing this!

Secrets of the Dead

Family Feuds

Viking families were easily offended. If someone insulted or annoyed a Viking, there was almost always a fight. If someone was killed, the victim's family took revenge and attacked the killer or his family. Then the other family fought back. These violent blood feuds went on and on until other Vikings had a meeting and decided who was at fault. At the meeting, they figured out who should pay a fine, called "blood-money," to the other side.

Answer: These are ice skates made from bone. Vikings shaped the bones into a wedge and then made holes in them so they could tie the skates to their feet using leather straps.

23

LONGHOUSES AND STALE STEWS

Viking homes were called longhouses. "Long-rooms" would have been a better name because these large buildings had only one room. They had to be long because several **generations** of one family shared the space.

Every longhouse had a large, open fire in the middle. This was used for cooking and heating. It filled the place with smoke. In cold winters, the family usually slept on benches at one end of the house. Their slaves and farm animals slept on the ground at the other end.

With so many people living, sleeping, and eating together with animals nearby inside one room, a Viking longhouse would have been warm. It would also be very noisy and dirty.

Viking Longhouses

- Walls were built from wood, stone, or earth.
- Roofs were often covered with turf (soil and grass), which helped keep in the heat.
- Benches were made of wood and covered with dried heather for a mattress.
- Rugs were made from animal skins. Cushions were made from woven fabric stuffed with feathers.
- There were no windows so Vikings used whale-oil lamps to see.
- Vikings made wooden buckets for washing. They dug holes outside and put a plank across with a hole in it. This was used as a washroom.

Viking Stew

When Viking women cooked a meal, they made a **cauldron**-full! They left it bubbling away in the pot over a fire for days afterward. This stale, brown stew often consisted of boiled lamb bones, onions, carrots, turnips, and beans. Hungry Vikings mopped it up with tough bread made from rye or barley flour.

Some Vikings drank from drinking horns that were usually made from cleaned and polished cow horns.

Food and Drink

Vikings ate meat they hunted and farmed, and fish they caught in the sea. They ate eggs, nuts, berries, and vegetables. They drank cows' milk and used it to make cheese and butter. To make sure they had enough food to last over winter, they dried or smoked fish and meat, or rubbed it all over with salt. They drank from horns. They often decorated the horns, sometimes with metal ends.

25

VIKING JEWELRY
AND SCRATCHY TUNICS

Vikings loved their jewelry. Everyone except the slaves wore jewelry every day. Rich jarls wore the best jewelry. Their favorite pieces were made from silver and gold. Ordinary karls made their own jewelry from bronze, **pewter**, or animal bones.

Jewelry was not just for decoration or to show off wealth. Women used brooches with necklaces of colorful glass beads between them to attach their aprons to dresses. Men used a ring pin to fasten their cloaks.

This type of Viking brooch is known as a fibula. It is like a fancy modern safety pin.

Viking Fashion

A well-dressed Viking man wore a pair of woolen baggy pants and one or two long tunics pulled in at the waist by a leather belt. For example, Ragnar Shaggy-Trousers' wife made his pants from animal fur. Women wore long-sleeved dresses that went down to their ankles. They wore a pinafore over them. Children wore the same. In winter, Vikings also wore a wool or leather cloak for extra warmth. Viking shoes were made from leather. Some had laces to keep them on.

DEADly Secrets

The Vikings are often portrayed as a scruffy, dirty bunch. However, they took pride in their appearance. They used toothpicks, ear and nail cleaners, and combs like this one made from antler or bone. Vikings did not just use combs to untangle their long locks. What else do you think Vikings used combs for?

Hint: Vikings scratched their heads a lot! • • • • • • • • • •

Secrets of the Dead

How Vikings Made Clothes

- Vikings made rough, scratchy linen from the leaves of the flax plant. Wool came from sheep. It was women's work to spin the fibers, weave them into sheets of fabric, and then to cut up that fabric and sew it into clothes.
- Some clothes were worn in their natural colors of browns and grays. Others were dyed rich reds, yellows, and blues, using plants such as **woad**, **weld**, and **madder**.

Answer: The Vikings often had annoying head lice that made their scalp itch so they combed their hair a lot to get rid of the nits (lice eggs).

MAGIC RUNES AND COLORFUL SAGAS

We know about Vikings from what other people wrote about them. Icelandic sagas record the histories that Vikings used to tell each other. **Descendants** of the Vikings, who lived in Iceland up to 300 years later, wrote down these sagas.

Anglo-Saxon Chronicles are books about England's history written by monks. Although written at the same time as the Vikings lived, the monks were not fond of the Vikings so it is hard to know if they tell the whole truth.

Runes

The Vikings recorded some facts using 16 special **symbols** called **runes**. They believed the runes had magical powers. They carved runes into large stones to remember important people who had died.

Runestones were big. They were painted in bright colors so they would be noticed. The stones often stood near roads or bridges, where many people passed by.

Long Sagas about the Vikings

The Icelandic Sagas reveal another secret about the Vikings: that they went to North America! After settling in Greenland, some Vikings set off to explore the northeastern coast of North America in around CE 1000. The sagas reveal how these Vikings tried to settle in an area they named Vinland. However, they eventually gave up and abandoned this new territory.

This museum version of King Harald's famous Jelling stone, showing Christ on the cross, is painted in bright colors that help reveal the details of the engravings.

Vikings used rune carvings to tell the future, cast spells, and provide protection. Warriors used runes on their weapons to make them more powerful.

The End of the Vikings

The most famous Viking runestones are the huge Jelling Stones. King Harald Bluetooth of Denmark and Norway had these runestones made between CE 965 and 985 in memory of his mother and father. They also give us a clue as to what happened to the Vikings. There is a figure of Christ on the cross on the stone. Harald was proud of making his people become Christians. By the 1100s, most Vikings had settled down, become Christians, and forgotten their old gods. The age of the mighty Vikings was over.

GLOSSARY

abbey place where monks and nuns live

afterlife life after death, or the idea that there is another world people live in after they die

altar table or surface used for a religious ritual

amulet small item worn for good luck or to ward off evil

archaeologist person who digs up and studies the remains of ancient cultures

artifact object made by a human being that has cultural or religious importance

blacksmith person who makes and repairs things in iron, with a fire and some tools

blood feud long-running fight between families, who kill each other for revenge for other killings

bronze strong metal made from a mixture of melted metals, such as copper and tin

cauldron large pot used for boiling

descendant someone who is related to a person or group of people who lived in the past

figurehead wooden carving at the front of a ship

fossilized resin juice from a tree that hardened millions of years before to become a beautiful brown gem

generation people in a family born and living during the same time

ivory tusk or giant tooth

madder plant that gives a dark reddish-purple dye

monastery building or group of buildings where monks live

monk man who has joined a religious community and promised to live a simple life

narwhal Arctic toothed whale that has a black-spotted whitish skin. Males have a long spiral tusk

natural resource useful material found in nature

navigate find one's way

Norse language of ancient Norway, Sweden, Denmark, and Iceland

offering something that is given as part of a religious ritual

pewter metal made of lead and copper

plunder loot or steal by force

ritual action or set of actions done over and over again for a special purpose, often connected to a person's religion or belief

rune character in the Viking alphabet

sacrifice kill an animal or person to please a god in a religious ceremony

Scandinavia group of countries made up of Denmark, Norway, and Sweden

slave person who is owned by someone else and forced to work without pay

symbol something that represents or stands for something else

weld plant that gives a yellow dye

woad plant that gives a blue dye

READ MORE

Books

Deary, Terry. *Vicious Vikings* (Horrible Histories). New York: Scholastic, 2013.

Ganeri, Anita. *How to Live Like a Viking Warrior* (How to Live Like…). Minneapolis, MN: Hungry Tomato, 2015.

Higgins, Nadia. *Everything Vikings* (Everything Series). Washington, D.C.: National Geographic Kids, 2015.

Raum, Elizabeth. *What Did the Vikings Do for Me?* (Linking the Past and Present). North Mankato, MN: Heinemann, 2011.

Ridley, Sarah. *Life in Viking Times* (Everyday History). Collingwood, Canada: Smart Apple Media, 2016.

Web Sites

Explore the world of the Vikings:
www.dkfindout.com/us/history/vikings

Watch this video to learn interesting facts about the Vikings:
www.history.com/topics/exploration/vikings-history/videos/bet-you-didnt-know-vikings

Discover lots more about the Vikings at:
http://jorvik-viking-centre.co.uk/who-were-the-vikings

Visit a Viking training school at:
www.nms.ac.uk/explore/play/discover-the-vikings/vikings-training-school

INDEX